HERE COME T
★ HARLEM ★
GLOBETROTTERS®

by Larry Dobrow

Ready-to-Read

Simon Spotlight

New York   London   Toronto   Sydney   New Delhi

SIMON SPOTLIGHT
An imprint of Simon & Schuster Children's Publishing Division
1230 Avenue of the Americas, New York, New York 10020
This Simon Spotlight edition August 2017
© 2017 Copyright Harlem Globetrotters International, Inc.
SIMON SPOTLIGHT, READY-TO-READ, and colophon are registered trademarks of Simon & Schuster, Inc.
For information about special discounts for bulk purchases, please contact Simon & Schuster Special Sales at
1-866-506-1949 or business@simonandschuster.com.
Manufactured in the United States of America 0119 LAK
4 6 8 10 9 7 5 3
This book has been cataloged with the Library of Congress.
ISBN 978-1-4814-8746-7 (hc)
ISBN 978-1-4814-8745-0 (pbk)
ISBN 978-1-4814-8747-4 (eBook)

CONTENTS

CHAPTER 1: THE GLOBETROTTERS STORY   4

CHAPTER 2: THE GLOBETROTTERS WAY   11

CHAPTER 3: THE GLOBETROTTERS PLAYERS   16

CHAPTER 4: THE GLOBETROTTERS UNIVERSE   32

CHAPTER 1
The Globetrotters Story

Legendary skills. Unbeatable athleticism. All-around fun. For more than ninety years the Harlem Globetrotters have been dazzling fans both on and off the basketball court. They have appeared with Olympians and world leaders, broken countless records, and brought basketball to places where it had never before been played. There simply isn't any other team like the Harlem Globetrotters. But how did this team become what it is today? Read on to find out!

The Harlem Globetrotters were founded way back in 1926, but they weren't called the Harlem Globetrotters at first. They were called the Savoy Big Five. The Savoy Ballroom was a well-known dance hall in Chicago. But what did a dance hall have to do with basketball? Nothing, actually! The ballroom's owners supported the team in the hope that fans would visit the Savoy for food and dancing after the games.

The man behind the team was Abe Saperstein. While he didn't play for the

Globetrotters, he did just about everything else, including coaching and scheduling. He even hand-sewed the team's first uniforms!

On January 7, 1927, the team played their first game on the road in Hinckley, Illinois, about fifty miles away from Chicago. But even though the team was from Chicago, what was written on the

players' uniforms? "New York." They wanted people to think they were from there. Soon "New York" was replaced with "Harlem," a famous neighborhood in New York City. The team also began using the term "Globe Trotters" to give fans the impression that they played all over the world. After some years the name finally stuck. They were officially the Harlem Globetrotters, and they were indeed about to travel the world.

GLOBETROTTERS FOR THE WIN!

The team won its first World Basketball Championship in 1940 and won the International Cup in 1943 and 1944.

The Globetrotters' first overseas trip took place in 1950. On that tour the team played games in nine countries: Portugal, Switzerland, England, Belgium, France, Germany, Italy, Morocco, and Algeria. Since 1950 the Harlem Globetrotters have traveled to 122 countries or territories on six continents. The only continent they still have to visit: Antarctica!

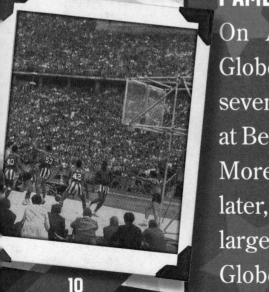

FAME AROUND THE WORLD

On August 22, 1951, the Globetrotters played before seventy-five thousand fans at Berlin's Olympic Stadium. More than sixty-five years later, this still stands as the largest crowd to attend a Globetrotters' game.

CHAPTER 2:
The Globetrotters Way

Every Globetrotter is a professional athlete, but not every professional athlete can be a Globetrotter. That's because Globetrotters must possess a unique combination of traits. Beyond athletic skill, Globetrotters must be great entertainers, dazzling the audience with amazing basketball feats and making them laugh. And most importantly, a Harlem Globetrotter must be an ambassador of goodwill. An **ambassador** is someone who represents or promotes a certain group or ideal to the rest of the world. The Globetrotters have spent decades promoting sportsmanship, service, and smiles throughout the world.

The Globetrotters have been known as ambassadors of goodwill since 1952. They visited places that few other American organizations would go, like Eastern Europe in the late 1950s and early 1960s. At that time, there was tension between that region and the United States.

When Lynette Woodard joined the Globetrotters in 1985, she became the first female player on the team. She wasn't the last, either. Fifteen women have suited up for the Globetrotters since then. In addition to being the first female Globetrotter, Woodard was the captain of the gold medal–winning US women's basketball team in the 1984 Olympics, and she played in the first two seasons of the WNBA from 1997 to 1999!

And as much as the Globetrotters love playing on the court, they love giving back off the court even more. Every year the players visit more than 150 hospitals worldwide, bringing smiles to the children there. They even use special basketballs to raise awareness for causes or to honor people. In 2015 they played with a camouflage ball to honor members of the US military.

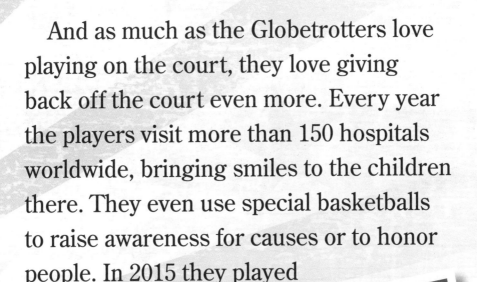

CHAPTER 3:
The Globetrotters Players

Seven Globetrotters have had their numbers retired by the team, which means that no other Globetrotter player will ever wear that number again. Those seven legendary players are:

Wilt Chamberlain (#13): Before he went on to become one of the greatest players in NBA history, Chamberlain played a full season with the Harlem Globetrotters.

Even as he racked up record after record in the NBA, he continued to rejoin the Globetrotters between NBA seasons.

Charles "Tex" Harrison (#34): In the six decades that Harrison played for or coached the Harlem Globetrotters, he visited more than one hundred countries. He even had tea with the queen of England! He once said, "Aside from my family, being a Harlem Globetrotter has been the greatest highlight of my life."

Marques Haynes (#20): Haynes logged two stints with the Globetrotters, one in the 1940s/1950s and the other in the 1970s. He was most famous for his dribbling skills and was said to be the fastest of any player of his era.

Meadowlark Lemon (#36): With his on-court antics, Lemon was known as the "clown prince of basketball." Over the course of twenty-four years with the team, he played in more than 7,500 consecutive games.

Fred "Curly" Neal (#22): One of the team's greatest ball handlers and shooters, Neal played twenty-two seasons for the Globetrotters. His time with the team spanned more than six thousand games in ninety-seven different countries.

Reece "Goose" Tatum (#50): Tatum was a baseball star before he ever set foot on the basketball court as a Globetrotter. He is remembered as a showman and an innovator. He was so incredible at the hook shot that he could make one without even looking! He was also a very large man. His fingertip-to-fingertip arm span was reported to be eighty-four inches. That's the size of a person who stands seven feet tall!

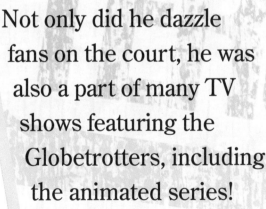

Hubert "Geese" Ausbie (#35): Ausbie played on the Globetrotters for twenty-four years. An amazing athlete, he chose playing for the Globetrotters over playing baseball for the Chicago Cubs. Not only did he dazzle fans on the court, he was also a part of many TV shows featuring the Globetrotters, including the animated series!

Many Globetrotters or those associated with the Globetrotters have been inducted into the Naismith Memorial Basketball Hall of Fame, including Abe Saperstein, Lynette Woodard, Wilt Chamberlain, Marques Haynes, Meadowlark Lemon, Mannie Jackson, Zack Clayton, and Goose Tatum. Some other Hall of Famers include:

William "Pop" Gates: A player and coach in basketball's pre-NBA era and a Globetrotter player/coach for five seasons.

Nathaniel "Sweetwater" Clifton: Clifton was a Globetrotter for two seasons before he became the first African-American player to sign a contract with an NBA team, the New York Knicks, in 1950.

Connie Hawkins: An NBA, ABA, and ABL star who played four seasons with the Globetrotters.

Finally, the team itself was inducted into the Hall of Fame in 2002!

GLOBETROTTERS FOR THE WIN!

Until 1950, the NBA was not integrated, which means that African Americans were not allowed on NBA teams. The Globetrotters helped break that color barrier when they defeated the NBA's Minneapolis Lakers two years in a row in 1948 and 1949.

And what about the players who make up today's team? Current stars include:

ANTHONY "ANT" ATKINSON (#12): Ant delivers some of the Globetrotters' best lines—and some of their most incredible records. He holds three team records: ninety-three points scored in a single game, most four-pointers in a single quarter, and twenty-two four-point shots in one game.

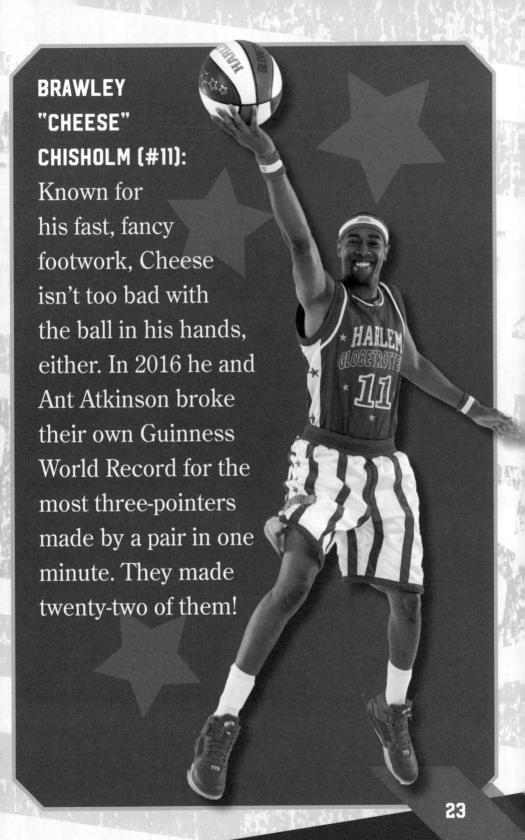

BRAWLEY "CHEESE" CHISHOLM (#11): Known for his fast, fancy footwork, Cheese isn't too bad with the ball in his hands, either. In 2016 he and Ant Atkinson broke their own Guinness World Record for the most three-pointers made by a pair in one minute. They made twenty-two of them!

CRISSA "ACE" JACKSON (#1): Ace might stand only five feet four inches tall, but that hasn't stopped her from becoming one of the team's most skilled shooters and playmakers.

COREY "THUNDER" LAW (#34): Since joining the Globetrotters, Thunder has set the Guinness World Record for the longest shot made while sitting down (58 feet, 9.12 inches). He also has the Guinness World Record for the longest shot made under one leg (52 feet, 5.5 inches)!

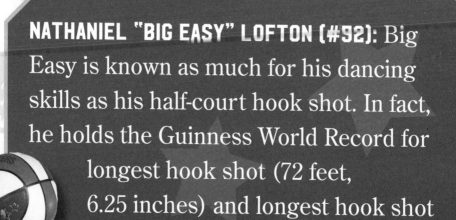

NATHANIEL "BIG EASY" LOFTON (#52): Big Easy is known as much for his dancing skills as his half-court hook shot. In fact, he holds the Guinness World Record for longest hook shot (72 feet, 6.25 inches) and longest hook shot blindfolded (58 feet, 2.5 inches).

FATIMA "TNT" LISTER (#18): When TNT joined the Globetrotters in 2011, she became the first female player on the team in nearly twenty years. Incredibly, she didn't start playing basketball until she was thirteen years old. Most professional basketball players start when they are five or six!

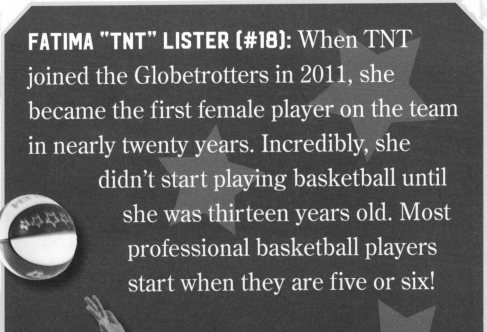

KRIS "HI-LITE" BRUTON (#26): Hi-Lite didn't make his first slam dunk until he was a senior in high school, but that didn't stop him from achieving his dreams. As a Globetrotter, Hi-Lite has played basketball on military aircraft carriers and even on ice in Central Park, New York City!

WILL "BULL" BULLARD (#33): In addition to playing basketball, Bull Bullard loves writing poetry. He's also not afraid of heights! In 2016 he made a shot from 110 feet in the air on a thrill ride at the New Jersey shore!

JONTE "TOO TALL" HALL (#7): Too Tall holds quite an impressive record: At five feet two inches tall, he is the shortest Globetrotter of all time. He loves art and singing.

CHRIS "HANDLES" FRANKLIN (#14): Handles has wanted to be a Globetrotter since he watched their television show when he was a child. These days he holds the Guinness World Record for the farthest backwards basketball shot made while kneeling, at 60 feet, 7.5 inches.

GLOBETROTTERS FOR THE WIN!

The Harlem Globetrotters currently hold sixteen Guinness World Records in basketball. The most unusual one? Scooter Christensen (#16) holds the record for spinning a basketball on his nose for the longest amount of time (7.7 seconds).

CHAPTER 4:
The Globetrotters Universe

Most fans have seen the Harlem Globetrotters on the basketball court, but the team has been seen in many other venues as well. In the 1950s the Globetrotters appeared in two movies: *The Harlem Globetrotters* and *Go, Man, Go!* On television, the Globetrotters, or animated versions of them, starred in a pair of Saturday morning cartoons. In one of those cartoons, the "Super Globetrotters" were superheroes fighting crime. Players for the team have also appeared on *The Amazing Race*, *American Ninja Warrior*, and *Sesame Street*.

The Globetrotters haven't confined their games to typical basketball courts, either. Over the years the team has played games in baseball stadiums, aircraft carriers, and on mountaintops. They have played games on ice, in the rain, and even in the dark—using a glow-in-the-dark basketball, of course!

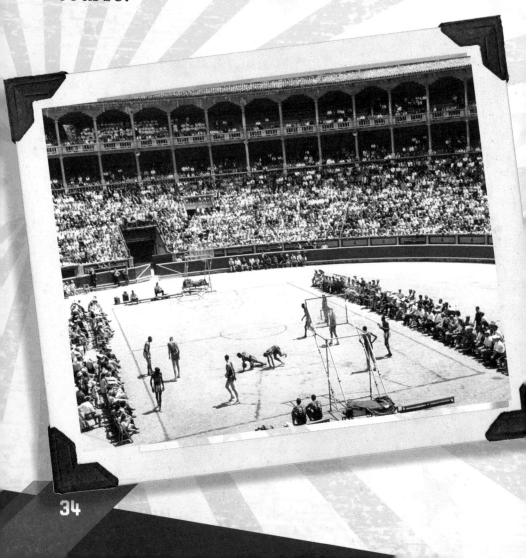

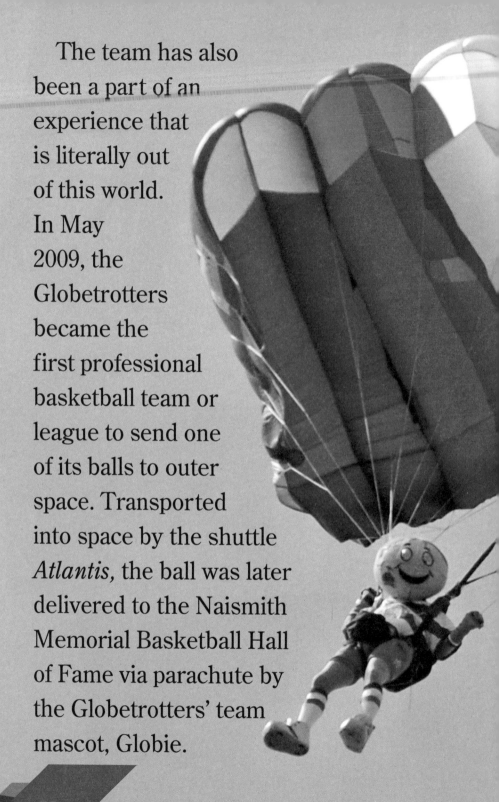

The team has also been a part of an experience that is literally out of this world. In May 2009, the Globetrotters became the first professional basketball team or league to send one of its balls to outer space. Transported into space by the shuttle *Atlantis,* the ball was later delivered to the Naismith Memorial Basketball Hall of Fame via parachute by the Globetrotters' team mascot, Globie.

Even today, the Globetrotters are still changing the game of basketball. In 2010 the team debuted the first four-point shot in the history of professional basketball. In 2017 they introduced the four-point line, which sits thirty feet away from the basket. That's six feet and three inches farther than the three-point line used in the NBA.

Now that you've met the Harlem Globetrotters, where do you think they will go next?

THE GLOBETROTTERS GO TO HOLLYWOOD!

On January 19, 1982, the Globetrotters became the first sports team honored with its own star on the Hollywood Walk of Fame.

THE ORIGINAL HARLEM GLOBETROTTERS

#1 ACE JACKSON · #2 DIZZY ENGLISH · #3 FIREFLY FISHER · #4 FLIGHT TIME LANG · #6 HOOPS GREEN · #7 TOO TALL HALL · #8 ROCKET PENNINGTON · #11 CHEESE CHISHOLM · #12 ANT ATKINSON · #14 HANDLES FRANKLIN · #15 BUCKETS BLAKES · #16 SCOOTER CHRISTENSEN · #17 SWISH YOUNG · #18 TNT LISTER · #19 FLIP WHITE · #23 BEAST DOUGLAS · #24 DRAGON TAYLOR · #26 HI-LITE BRUTON · #30 ZEUS McCLURKIN · #31 HAMMER HARRISON · #32 JET RIVERS · #33 BULL BULLARD · #34 THUNDER LAW · #38 JUMPIN' JOE BALLA · #39 EL GATO MELENDEZ · #40 SLICK WILLIE SHAW · #42 SPIDER SHARPLESS · #44 WUN "THE SHOT" VERSHER · #45 MOOSE WEEKES · #48 CLUTCH BALL · #52 BIG EASY LOFTON · COACHES: SWEET LOU DUNBAR · JIMMY BLACKLOCK · BA...